SUMMARY
& ANALYSIS

OF

THE ENERGY
CODES

The 7-Step System to Awaken Your
Spirit, Heal Your Body, and Live
Your Best Life

A GUIDE TO THE BOOK
BY DR. SUE MORTER

NOTE: This book is a summary and analysis and is meant as a companion to, not a replacement for, the original book.

Please follow this link to purchase a copy of the original book: https://amzn.to/2ICmsLR

TABLE OF CONTENTS

SYNOPSIS

In her book, *The Energy Codes: The 7-Step System to Awaken Your Spirit, Heal Your Body, and Live Your Best Life*, Dr. Sue Morter reveals the energy-based practices that anyone can use to overcome chronic pain, depression, and other physical and mental conditions and feel a powerful sense of purpose, fulfillment, and love every day.

Drawing from years of research and practice, Morter details how we can look beyond our default human condition—with all its disease and suffering—and come to a full awareness of the true greatness that lies within us. This transformation, she contends, begins when we recognize that our physicality is only part of us; our spirit, the pure energy within us, is our true self. When we live into the true reality of our lives, we open ourselves up to deep universal wisdom and settle into our constant inner state of wholeness and perfection.

The Energy Codes is divided into three parts. The first part makes the case that we are energy beings passing through a physical dimension to discover our limitless power. Each chapter of the second part explains one of the seven energy codes and describes the practices that increase the presence of the essential energy within us. The third part ties everything together and shows what it is like to live as the Soulful Self, or spirit.

INTRODUCTION

For the better part of her life, Sue Morter was an overachiever. She was the cheerleader in her high school, and she won "best actress" in state drama competitions.

However, despite her achievements, she struggled with feelings of inadequacy. So much so that the professional and financial success she attained by her mid-thirties felt joyless and unfulfilling.

Sue knew about the infinite energy in the universe. She suspected it was the way to a fuller and more meaningful life. Her father, Dr. M. T. Morter Jr., was a chiropractic doctor and a pioneer in "energy medicine." Sue started her career working with him in his healthcare practice. She went on to become a licensed chiropractor and her father's partner in energy research.

Sue was never really aware of this infinite energy until one day, while meditating in a darkened room full of hundreds of other meditators, she felt weightless and perceived a radiance coming from within her. Her breath, she recounts, flowed like a loving presence from within her to the earth beneath her. At that moment, she found respite from the weight of her demanding life and, for the first time, felt whole and complete.

Meditation shifted her perspective of what was real and brought her out of the pain and suffering she had accepted as an inevitable part of life. It made her realize that her problems were essential tools in her spiritual journey. When she surrendered to the calmness and energy within her, she became healthier and happier. Her migraines disappeared, and she lost her visceral need to prove herself. Instead, she began to trust the timing of her life's circumstances. She sought fulfillment rather than success, and success came as a consequence.

PART I: A NEW WAY OF SEEING—THE QUANTUM FLIP

CHAPTER 1: PROJECT AWAKENING: SHIFTING FROM PAIN TO BLISS

How much pain or bliss you experience depends on the truth you know about yourself. It depends on how much you know and live from the knowledge that you are conscious energy.

Morter draws from her experience to illustrate the power of this knowledge. When her father passed away, he left his entire estate to her two brothers. Sue had worked with him for years and was by his hospital bed when he died. Being cut out of his will felt like the worst kind of rejection she could experience.

Sue was just about to lead the first session of a women's retreat when her brother emailed her a copy of their father's will. The pain of being cut off the will crushed her, and she wondered if she could go on stage.

When she began to apply the Energy Codes she had been developing, she aligned her shattered energy, calmed her body down, and felt feelings of safety and peace return to her. Without the knowledge of the power she had to alter her energy, she would have taken being cut out to mean that something was wrong with her. She admits that she might have withdrawn from her family and abandoned her life's work.

Key Takeaway: Everything in the universe, including human beings, is pure, intelligent energy.

The physical world we experience is not really physical; it is all energy that has been compressed so densely that we can perceive it with our five senses. Matter is no different from light waves, sound waves, and other forms of energy. Thoughts are also a form of energy.

Nearly every problem you have can be tied back to the belief that you are your body and mind. This belief is toxic because it obscures your true nature. For as long as you identify as your body and mind, you will never feel whole; there will always be something about your looks, intellect, finances, or relationships that feels wrong or is missing. You will never shake off this feeling until you awake to the fact that your true essence is pure, unlimited energy.

"Our problem as humans isn't that we are inadequate, wrong, or broken; our problem is that we believe we are" (Morter, p. 16).

Key Takeaway: Living as your Soulful Self is the antidote to your feelings of inadequacy and aloneness.

There is a version of you that is whole and perfect. It is your Soulful Self, the source of the infinite energy within you.

Until you become aware of yourself as an energy form, you live from your ego or Protective Personality. From the perspective of this identity, you are separate, alone, and unsafe. When you identify as your body and mind, you separate yourself from others, nature, and your essential energy, your true self. You find that you are always on guard against anything that threatens the smaller egotistic identity you are living from and the story you tell yourself about who you are, and you are always looking for acceptance and approval.

Your journey to wholeness begins when you see yourself as pure, unlimited energy. When you live from your Soulful Self, you focus inward—rather than outward—on the energy within you and let it guide you to your true path. You feel open and connected to everything, opportunities for love and growth come naturally, and life becomes effortless. When your spirit leads the way, you can bend life to your will.

Key Takeaway: Awakening to your Soulful Self is evolution through three levels of consciousness.

You are here to awaken your Soulful Self. Everything that has happened to you has been moving you closer to this self. When you understand how awakening works, you can shift into your Soulful Self with more ease and speed.

The shift from the Protective Personality to the Soulful Self occurs in stages. In the first stage (survival/victimhood stage), you see life as something that happens to you. You resign yourself to your circumstances because you feel you have no control over them.

In the second stage (self-help stage), you become aware that you are in pain and open up to the possibility that you don't have to be. You still see life as something that happens to you, but you are aware that you can control your experience of it. You begin to look for the change that will make you happier, healthier, and fulfilled.

In the third stage (creatorship stage), you realize that there is no bad circumstance to fix or silver lining to find because every challenge you encounter is meant to serve your growth. You see life as something that happens for you— and always for the benefit of your growth—and discover, at a deeper level, that you purposely willed your circumstances into existence to discover your limitless power.

Knowing that you are a creator, you engage more deeply with the flow of life and become more grateful. When you are fully tuned to your Soulful Self, devastating circumstances no longer generate the pain they used to.

Key Takeaway: Embody the energy you are to live your fullest life.

We are more than spiritual beings with physical experiences; we are spiritual beings with spiritual experiences living in a physical but energy-filled world.

To live into your Soulful or Spirit Self, you must bring your energy to life. When you build new circuitry, establish a natural flow of energy in your body, and anchor to this eternal energy, you can make a quantum flip from living as your Protective Personality to your Soulful Self.

Embodying the energy that you are opens up access to your intuition, and this intuition guides you to a creative, fulfilling life.

CHAPTER 2: YOUR ROLE IN CREATING YOUR LIFE

Each type of energy has a unique wavelength and vibrates at a different frequency. Pure light, for example, takes up the highest frequencies. Sound, thoughts, and emotions are just energy forms with different vibrational frequencies.

The different circulatory systems in the body have unique frequencies, as do the different cells, molecules, and atoms of each organ.

Key Takeaway: Everything in the universe is interconnected.

Since everything is energy, there is no empty space in the universe, and nothing exists in isolation. Everything is interconnected in infinite layers of energy.

Your mere presence, as illustrated by the double-split experiment, affects atoms, which are the building blocks of the universe. Your actions and emotions affect your internal mechanisms and every area of your life. Negative emotions such as anger, for example, can compress DNA molecules. Positive emotions such as love can expand these molecules.

As an energy form, you have a personal energy field that changes with your internal behaviors and the things you interact with in your external environment. Modern technologies such as electroencephalography (EEG) and superconducting quantum interference devices (SQUIDs) can measure and monitor this energy field.

Changes in your energy field also affect your health. Physiological symptoms that appear when you are unwell are actually symptoms of disturbance in your biofield. If your spiritual body energy is activated, you can experience miraculous healing in your physical and emotional body. The goal of awakening is to bring the highest vibration of conscious energy into the physical body.

Key Takeaway: Your energy field reflects the reality of your life.

Your energy field vibrates in different ways depending on what you are doing, thinking, and feeling. It can be vital and bright when you are immersed in an inspiring conversation and dull and small when you are thinking about the responsibilities you hate. Your energy may look dispersed on the surface of your field if you feel victimized, fearful, or if you are going through judgment, rejection, or trauma. It can appear to be flowing and centered on your core if you are living closer to your Soulful Self.

Anything that overwhelms or upsets you, any outcome that you feel is undesirable to you, is a blockage that splatters your energy and inhibits its flow. The more blockages you have, the more your energy is dispersed, and the more you seek fulfillment from external sources. The more dispersed your energy is, the more disappointments you encounter, and the more painful your experience of life becomes.

Conversely, the more you embrace the circumstances of your life, the more your energy is unified and integrated, and the more you experience a full life. When your energy is unified, you feel in control, at ease and happy.

Problems in any area of your life are a sign of energy interferences in that area. If you have blockages in your mental or emotional layer, for example, you will feel unmotivated, disillusioned, and isolated. Blockages in the mental or emotional layer can lead to physical injury and disease because interferences in one layer affect the layers beneath it.

Key Takeaway: You create your reality.

You direct and manage your energy flows with your thoughts, the foods you eat, and the relationships you have with other people. Your experiences affect your energy, and your energy shapes your experiences. It is this pattern of cause and effect that creates your reality. You create your reality from the inside out: from your energy to your external world.

When you are living from your ego or Protective Personality, your mind is focused on the external world. Since energy follows your focus, it scatters outward and away from the core. The more you focus outside yourself, the more your energy becomes fragmented or blocked, and the more your reality seems bleak.

When you turn your focus inward, your energy follows this focus and concentrates on your core. Consequently, you begin to feel grounded and whole.

Key Takeaway: You are constantly evolving.

The universe is continually evolving, and every person's consciousness evolves with it. Everything that happens in life is in furtherance of this evolution. Even the things that undermine your wellbeing or that seem to serve no purpose are part of this evolution.

If you were a spirit being passing through the earth to experience a physical dimension that would help reveal more of your true self, you would want to have experiences that stretched you to your limits. If you wanted to experience unconditional forgiveness, for example, you would ask that another being do something that would cause you untold pain and suffering, then see if you could forgive them. If someone caused you this untold pain, you would appreciate it for what it was—an undesirable circumstance you created for yourself to advance your spiritual evolution.

Awakening is not about making the best of a bad situation; it is recognizing that the bad situation, which you, a spirit being, wished on yourself for your journey through this physical dimension, is there to help you explore a deeper and truer part of you of which you were previously unaware. Your most devasting circumstance is not something you would choose, but it is happening *for* you.

Experiences of extreme loss, abuse, and illness that seem impossible to get through are big projects for big beings. It takes these big challenges to reveal the magnificence of a big soul.

CHAPTER 3: THE INVISIBLE YOU: BIOENERGY BASICS

Being pure energy, which can neither be created nor destroyed, all of humanity has always been and will always be here in the universe.

When we get on this physical plane, we are unaware of our true identity as spirits. We develop the Protective Personality, a false self, to orient ourselves to the world. We come up with stories to make sense of the world and our circumstances. These stories limit us because they do not reflect our true identity.

Your task here is to unify your dispersed energy and remember who you really are—a spirit being with a physical body, but otherwise complete and whole. Living at the energy level of being—the level beyond thoughts, feelings, emotions, and physicality—is the way to freedom and happiness.

Key Takeaway: Look inward to begin healing yourself.

Your logical mind, as with anything physical, is limited in its ability to give you the answers you seek or guide you on your true path.

To heal your life, to be free and happy, you have to let your energy guide you, and you have to invite your mind to follow. You have to shift your awareness from the external world—from the stories you tell yourself and your attempts to fix things—and look inward and follow the flow of your energy. Rather than reacting to external circumstances, you act from the infinite wisdom of your true self.

Anything you experience in your physical or emotional body happens at the energy level first. The sensations you feel when something happens to you are actually shifts in your energy field. In this way, what harms and heals you comes from within you. Sickness does not merely come from viruses or other disease vectors, and healing does not just come from medicine and corrective surgery. Imbalances in your energy affect your health just as much, and true wholeness begins with remedial shifts in our energy fields.

Key Takeaway: Powerful energy is always flowing through you.

High-frequency universal energy flows from above the crown of your head, through a central channel in your system, down your feet, and into the earth, and is reflected back up again. This energic flow, which creates and regenerates your physical body, is your essence, your soul. It creates everything you experience as a physical being. You work with this energy to advance your evolution.

Seven energy centers that revolve around the spine—commonly known as Chakras—move this high-frequency energy through subdivisions of your body. Your essential energy encounters these rotating energy wheels as it flows through your body. It shoots out through the crown chakra at the top of your head and flows back into the root chakra at the base of your spine.

The energy state of each chakra determines how you perceive and perform in the area of your life to which that chakra relates. If there are blockages in your root chakra, for example, you will feel ungrounded and experience a sense of unbelonging. If one chakra is compromised, it might create problems with chakras above it, through which your energy rises. The more flow there is in the system, the clearer your reality is and the more wholeness you experience.

Key Takeaway: Energy interferences are more like gaps than blocks.

An energy blockage or interference is the result of the absence of a vital life force. If there is a spot in your biofield where your energy is not flowing, that spot lacks the animation or consciousness through which energy can flow. Your mind has not fully awakened your spirit, so your spirit is not alive and active at that spot.

Gaps in the flow of your energy are created when you encounter a situation you don't know how to deal with mentally or emotionally and, rather than go through it, you circumvent it and choose instead to hold on to something that gives you a false sense of safety. A person who has gone through trauma, for example, may shut herself off to trust and love as a coping mechanism. As long as this trauma goes unresolved, there will always be interference in her flow of energy. Complete physical, mental, and emotional healing occurs when all of your energy circuitry is activated.

PART II: A NEW WAY OF BEING—THE ENERGY CODES PROGRAM

CHAPTER 4: THE ANCHORING CODE: GETTING BACK IN YOUR BODY

The first step toward living as the Soulful Self is to anchor or concentrate your essential energy in your body.

The anchoring code brings you back to the body; it shifts your attention from the external world to your energetic core. When you unite your mind, body, and soul/breath, you begin to bring together your dispersed energy and awaken the healer in you. Consequently, you create more energy in your daily life and enjoy ease of mind and better physical and emotional health.

The anchoring code has a particular effect on your root chakra. This chakra governs your body's life force, well-being, and security. When it is inactive, you feel anxious and unstable, and you suffer through low vitality, weak immunity, and poor general health. Improving its function and flow increases your groundedness, physical energy, health, and self-mastery. Because this chakra is at the base of the central channel where high-frequency universal energy enters the body from the earth, its impairment affects the rest of the energy system.

A few yoga poses, done with focus and presence, can ground your energy and complement the benefits of the other exercises that bring your root chakra to life.

Squeezing the area around your root chakra while doing the poses and the practices recommended by Morter builds sensory awareness and integrates the energy in this area. This recommendation applies to the yoga poses and activation practices of the other chakras as well.

Key Takeaway: Maintain a conscious connection to your anchor points to embody your Soulful Self.

When you pull your focus and awareness inward, you engage with the world with a lot of power and energy because you are grounded. The four central channel anchor points you want to maintain are a conscious connection to your root chakra, heart center, throat, and third eye.

Morter provides specific exercises you can do to improve your conscious connection to the four anchor points. As some of the exercises may be complicated or difficult to understand, she directs readers to her website, drsuemorter.com, for a wealth of resources on practices, yoga, and meditation.

Key Takeaway: Use central channel breathing to awake your true essence.

Your breath is the way you move energy in and out of your energy field. You activate your chakras when you breathe through the core of your body and simultaneously maintain a conscious connection to your anchor points.

To practice central channel breathing, start by squeezing your pelvic floor, heart, and throat, and feeling the tension behind your eyes. Visualize your breath as a ball of light moving from a few inches above your head and down your central channel and into the earth. As you breathe, follow the ball of light down each energy center, squeezing and activating each anchor point along the path of your breath, and then back up again.

Every time you breathe from beyond and through your body, you activate your essential energy and come closer to the awareness that you are more than your physicality.

CHAPTER 5: THE FEELING CODE: THE LANGUAGE OF THE SOUL

Friction is essential to your growth. It shows you areas where your energy circuitry has not yet turned on. It shows you the places you need to awaken to live into your magical, Soulful Self. When someone says something that hurts you, for example, your system keeps you from moving on until you've reintegrated the energy that the situation dispersed. When you work with the bodily sensations the event caused, your energy shifts and the circuits affected open up. Since your mind follows your energy, it readjusts its perception of the event and moves on.

You don't have to wait for friction to advance your spiritual growth. You can pay attention to the energy shifts you experience when something happens and work through the message that they have for you. The aim is to feel the feeling in your body, not the emotion in your mind; it is to feel and sense more than you think and rationalize.

The second, or sacral, chakra is in charge of the emotional layer of your energy system. Integrating this chakra stabilizes your emotions so that you become less reactive and more attuned to your feelings. Disturbances in this chakra are the cause of lower digestive issues, unbalanced sex drive, distrust, anxiety, depression, and other physical, emotional, and mental health issues.

Key Takeaway: Shift your focus from the story in your mind to the sensations in your body to integrate your energy.

Any problems you experience in your physical, mental, or emotional state begin in your energy field. Working with the raw energy that makes your essence gives better and faster results than working through your symptoms.

When something happens, and you experience an emotional reaction, ask yourself where you feel it in your body rather than why it is happening to you. Feel the tightness, jittering, pain, or any other form of energy shift that accompanies your emotional reaction. Locate the part of your body where you feel the sensation and the chakra that it most closely corresponds to. Squeeze the muscles in the area of the sensation, do central channel breathing, "grabbing" that area with your mind as you breathe through it. Make one trip up and another trip down the channel. Practice until you feel a shift in your energy. This exercise communicates to your consciousness that you are opening up the flow of energy in the affected part.

Key Takeaway: Focus on feeling rather than naming your symptoms.

Your stuck energies, like anything else in your life, increase in presence and realness when you focus on them. When you name the negative emotions that develop from an undesirable circumstance, the emotions intensify. Part of the problem is that, by naming the negative emotion, you attach a mental story to it and react to this story. Each story you construct to avoid feeling the pain makes it harder to resolve the issue.

To resolve your emotional frictions, feel the sensations they come with, focus on the part of your body affected, and do your central channel breathing through this area. All emotions are energies that operate at different frequencies. No emotion is better or worse off than the other, and all serve their purpose in the natural cycle of growth.

A physical disease is also a form of energy that recalls your attention to a spot in your energy field that needs to be activated. You can work through illness the same way you work through emotions. Lean into the pain instead of avoiding it or burying it with medications, bring it into your full awareness, and use your conscious focus and energy to resolve it.

Key Takeaway: Monitor changes in your energy field throughout the day to keep in touch with your Soulful Self.

When you monitor your energy field, you can manage your energy shifts before they escalate into negative emotions. Keeping tabs on your energy flow also keeps you attuned to the knowledge, inspirations, and creative impulses that your inner wisdom is always sending to your conscious mind.

To keep an eye on your inside state, do a central channel scan every day before you get out of bed, throughout the day, and just before you sleep. Take your attention through your central channel, from above your head to the tip of your spine, and take several central channel breaths as you do this. Notice any energy surges and sensations or any area you can't stay focused on. These are signs that there is a gap in the flow of energy in that area.

Key Takeaway: Shift your energy vibration to the 'have-it' frequency to manifest what you want.

The vibrational frequency of your energy determines what life gives you. Wanting and having have different, mutually exclusive frequencies. You cannot have or attract into your life what you want. To manifest anything in your life, you must create the vibrational frequencies you would get if you already had it.

To do this, close your eyes, focus on something you want, and notice the sensations in your body. Then imagine you already have it. Notice how your energy has changed. Practice recalling how it felt to have what you want and hold in your consciousness the vibration that came with the feeling for as long as you can.

CHAPTER 6: THE CLEARING CODE: THE HEALING POWER OF THE SUBCONSCIOUS

Thoughts and emotions that have not been processed accumulate and block the energetic flow. Consequently, these unprocessed thoughts and emotions cause bodily pain or dysfunction and limit the body's ability to heal. Accessing the thoughts and emotions hidden away in the subconscious and releasing them is the way to healing and wholeness.

The clearing code relates to the solar plexus—the third chakra—which is about three inches above the navel. This chakra sits at the core of the Self and is the power center of your energy field. Clearing this center enhances your ability to be open and accepting of circumstances. Since this chakra also governs the stomach, liver, spleen, and pancreas, integrating it with your energy helps heal gut-related issues, including chronic conditions such as diabetes and Crohn's disease.

Key Takeaway: Do the Morter March to reset your high-brain centers and clear unresolved issues in your subconscious.

When the subconscious is overwhelmed, it shuts the door between itself and the conscious. This cuts off communication between the two minds, so the subconscious remains unaware of any progress made on the crisis or trauma that forced it to shut itself off. Even after the friction is resolved, it keeps sending emergency-mode signals to the body.

The Morter March is one of the practices that helps clear unresolved patterns in the subconscious and the tensions they cause. This practice activates and unifies several brain centers and brain systems, including the sensory and motor cortex, the right and left side of the body, and the visual and respiratory centers. It also activates the cerebellum, which is the home of the subconscious memory.

To do the Morter March, start by standing straight and tall. Bring your awareness to your body. Step your right knee forward and take a lunge, then raise your left arm in front of you with the thumb pointed upward. Take your right arm back and down behind you with the thumb pointed downward. Either arm should be spread 45 degrees toward the ceiling and floor, respectively. Turn your head and look over your left arm to your left thumb. Close your right eye, take a deep belly breath, and hold. Focus on the feeling of acceptance, forgiveness, or love. Keep your inhale until you can no longer hold your breath, then exhale and step back.

Repeat on the other side to complete one cycle. Do four cycles.

CHAPTER 7: THE HEART CODE: THE UNIVERSAL SOLVENT

Love is not something you get from someone or something outside yourself. Love is the essence of your Soul. The things you like merely magnify its vibrations. You must anchor in and live in the vibrational frequency of love to fully connect with your Soulful Self and with others. You must make the shift from thinking about and trying to get love to embodying its vibration.

When you generate the feeling of love from within yourself, you feel loved all the time; you tap into a vibrational frequency that leads to genuine happiness and joy and radical healing. Love merges the body, mind, and soul into a single entity, and its energy transforms the energy of any problem and negative emotion.

The heart code is correlated with the fourth, or heart, chakra. Located at the center of the chest, this chakra is where the energies of the lower and upper chakras meet and integrate. Lack of flow in this energy center can lead to emotional and mental problems such as loneliness, anxiety, and depression, as well as physical symptoms in your circulatory and respiratory systems. When this energy center is activated, you become more present, nonjudging, compassionate, and appreciative of life.

Key Takeaway: Do the loving triage practice to connect with the unconditional love within you.

You can generate and receive love by allowing your mind to perceive the love that already exists within your core.

To do the loving triage practice, think of someone or something you love. As you picture this object of affection and feel the sensation of love it conjures, recognize that this object only brings love from within you; you are perceiving what is already inside you. Fill your senses with the image of this object, and focus on how you feel inside as you do.

Expand this feeling of love and let it overflow beyond the room you are in. Remember how this feels in your body. Place your hand on your heart and affirm that the love you feel is for you. Visualize the love dropping into your core and feel it fill every part of your body. As you squeeze your heart center to feel the energy of this love, breathe through your central channel and anchor points. Hold the feeling of love for several breaths.

Key Takeaway: Turn on the love vibration to increase your capacity to let go and heal.

Love is the catalyst to any form of physical, mental, or emotional transformation. Its vibrational energies integrate the energy dispersal that causes disease and speed up healing.

When you're in a situation that causes fear, anger, or any type of friction, notice how your body changes and squeeze the area you feel the tension or charge. Later, when the stress subsides, picture something or someone you love, add as much detail to this picture as possible, then turn up your feeling for that object until your love overflows. Memorize how this feels in your body. Breathe through the central channel several times and, while you are doing this, squeeze the area where you felt the tension. Allow the love energy within you to resolve the friction and build new circuitry in the tension area. Generate this loving presence whenever you need to let go of something or heal.

Key Takeaway: Practice seeing everything as love to transform your experience of life.

When you are on your death bed, you are going to look back on your life and realize that everything that happened to you—including the things that almost broke you—was essential to living the amazing life you lived.

You don't have to wait until your final days to realize the abundance of love. You can choose today to see everything that happens to you as an interplay of love, a map toward the awakening of your Soulful Self. When you take up this perspective, you find it easier to see, experience, and share love, and enhance your ability to heal and rejuvenate.

To practice seeing everything as love, bring to mind a challenging situation you are going through and ask yourself how your view of this situation would change if it were a gift to expand your capacity to love or forgive. Use the practices of loving triage and generate a loving presence to build new circuits. Ask yourself how you can use the experience of the challenging situation to love yourself and others more.

CHAPTER 8: THE BREATH CODE: THE POWER OF LIFE ITSELF

Your breath is your spirit. It is your life. You can bring more of life, spirit, and the Soulful Self—which is the same thing, really—into your physical body through conscious breathing. When you focus your mind on an area of your body and breathe into it, you increase the flow of energy in it and enhance the abilities and qualities of life it governs.

The breath code is correlated with the throat chakra, which is located at the base of the neck. This chakra governs your voice, breath, and the expression of your true creative nature. When energy is not flowing through this chakra, you may experience physical symptoms such as sore throat, thyroid issues, and chronic issues such as asthma. You may suffer through perfectionism, blocked creativity, and difficulties expressing your emotion and sharing deep truths.

Key Takeaway: Breathe into your chakras to connect the energies of the universe with the physical energies in your body.

Everything in the world is made of atoms, which are made of subatomic particles, which float in an infinite space. This space is filled with pure energy, or spirit. When you breathe with awareness, you enhance the flow of this energy and awaken your wholeness.

Central channel breathing enhances the flow of energy through the root and crown chakras and connects you to the energies of the universe. To enhance this connection, visualize a vertical channel running from above your head to below your feet. Squeeze the root, heart, throat, and crown chakras as you breathe deeply into your belly. Exhale through the root chakra and into the earth. In the next cycle, inhale from deep in the earth, up through the tip of your spine and into your belly, and exhale through the heart, throat, behind the eyes, and out through the top of your head.

Key Takeaway: Breathe space into your tissues to heal injuries and chronic pain and awake your unlimited capacities.

You can make your system come even more alive by breathing through the tiny energy channels that run through your body.

To do this, first visualize your body as consisting of three sections: from the feet to the top of the hips, from the top of the hips to top of the shoulders, and from the top of the shoulders to the top of the head. Contract the section from your feet to your hips and visualize yourself inhaling from below your feet through this area, as if you had a thousand energy straws sucking up a thick fluid. Exhale as you get to the mid-body section, but hold the contraction in the lower part of your body.

Contract this second section, which includes your arms, and the pull up the energy you were sucking from the earth. Exhale into the neck and continue holding the contraction in the first and second body sections.

Inhale and contract the final section, including the neck, face, and scalp, and pull the energy you are sucking to the top of your head. Exhale and feel the energy flow out of your body, then relax all sections. Repeat twice or thrice. This practice, which Morter calls the 'thousand tiny straws breath' clears the blockages that cause bodily pain.

CHAPTER 9: THE CHEMISTRY CODE: THE ALCHEMY OF EMBODIMENT

Your body produces the chemicals that govern cell function, including hormones and enzymes, based on the information it receives from your energy field. Your physical body and energy field are entangled in an intricate feedback loop, so your energy influences your chemistry and your chemistry affects your energy. Your energy is at its peak when your body chemistry is at its best.

The chemistry code is correlated with the Third Eye, or the sixth chakra. Located between and above your eyebrows, this energy center programs for intuition, inspiration, and higher wisdom. It is associated with the pineal and pituitary glands, which manage the chemistry of the body and the awakening of consciousness. Proper nutrition and conscious exercise activate these glands and stabilizes the sixth chakra. Integrating this energy centers develops your sixth sense.

If this chakra is blocked, you may find it difficult to tune in to the signals from your body and trust your inner wisdom. You may also suffer through physical and mental symptoms such as headaches, dizziness, poor vision, depression, and addiction.

Key Takeaway: Create alkaline body chemistry to avoid and reverse chronic illnesses.

Your body chemistry is at the center of most diseases, and it determines the ease with which you heal. 95 percent of all diseases—including high blood pressure, osteoporosis, diabetes, and cancer—occur when the body is continuously in an acidic state. Cellular healing cannot occur in this state.

An alkaline body environment is necessary for optimal cell function and energy flow. It enhances the ease with which you manifest your desires, connect with your Soulful Self, and transform.

To create this healthy cellular environment, you must take foods that produce alkaline byproducts more than those that produce acidic byproducts. The foods that produce alkalinity in the body when metabolized are mostly fruits and vegetables. Acidifying foods include animal protein, dairy, grains, caffeine, sugar and sugary drinks, and highly processed foods.

To create an optimal alkaline body environment, fresh fruits and vegetables should make up 75 to 80 percent of your diet. Less than 25 percent of your diet should be meats and grains.

Your food combinations are as important as the types of food you eat. Eat protein with vegetables rather than starches, starches with vegetables, fruit by itself, and avoid dairy. These guidelines will enhance digestion, increase alkaline reserves in the body, and ease allergies, muscle pain, joint inflammation, and other types of chronic conditions.

Key Takeaway: Your thoughts affect your body chemistry more than your diet.

Your body chemistry is determined by more than the foods you eat; it is also determined by the air you breathe, chemicals you absorb, as well as your thoughts, emotions, and beliefs. You can be on an alkalinizing diet but end up with an acidic body condition because of your conscious or unconscious thoughts.

Thoughts that lead to high-frequency emotions, such as joy and love, produce feel-good chemicals that create an alkaline condition in the body. Thoughts and subconscious patterns that generate low-frequency emotions such as anger create acidifying chemicals. A prolonged pattern of worry can create more body acid than any alkaline diet can neutralize.

Key Takeaway: Focus on positive, high-frequency thoughts and reframe negative thoughts to cultivate alkaline body chemistry.

Begin your practice with central channel breathing. Focus on a moment in your life when you overcame a significant challenge. Notice how your energy changes and flows as you focus on this event in detail. Gently squeeze the area where you feel your energy moving to bring conscious awareness to it. Breathe through your central channel until that vibrational sensation flows through your entire system. This practice brings your whole system to the same positive vibrational frequency. You can tune into vibrations of inspiration, love, and joy the same way.

CHAPTER 10: THE SPIRIT CODE: WHERE THE MANY BECOME ONE

You begin to live as the Soulful Self when you train your mind to understand that you are a tangible spirit being. You go beyond perceiving and managing your energy to realizing you are the energy. The goal of the spirit code is to help you make the Quantum Flip: to get your mind and spirit to be so in harmony that they become one. This way, your Soul can direct your mind and body, and you can engage with life powerfully and lovingly.

The spirit code is correlated with the seventh, or crown, chakra. Integrating this chakra, which is the link to the non-physical dimension, catalyzes the shift from living in the constant barrage of thoughts run by your Protective

Personality to the think-less superconscious of the Soulful Self. You drop your egotistic self-image—together with its insecurity and self-doubt—and become present, open, and at peace with everything. When this chakra is not integrated, you feel you are separate from others and spirit, and you find yourself trapped in ego battles that lead to anxiety and depression.

Key Takeaway: Practice meditation to train your mind to listen to your Soulful Self.

To live into your best life, your mind has to serve your Soulful Self constantly and consistently. Your mind's job is not to run a train of thoughts all the time; it is to listen to what your Soulful Self—the real you—has to reveal.

When you quiet your mind in a meditation session, you allow your Soulful Self to rise from within. You dial down the reactivity of your mind so you can choose what to pay attention to in your outer world. Regular meditation practice of about twenty minutes a day stops the constant flow of thoughts so you can experience the presence of the real you.

To meditate, set a timer and sit comfortably. Take some deep belly breathes and squeeze the four anchor points (root, heart, throat, and eyes). Switch to slow central channel breathes for the rest of your practice. Focus on how your breath feels for the duration of your meditation. Observe thoughts as they come to mind, and tell your mind you will think about what it is bringing up later.

PART III: A NEW WAY OF LIVING—THE EMBODIED LIFE

CHAPTER 11: MAKING THE QUANTUM FLIP, ONE DAY AT A TIME

If there is a habit that can make the most difference in your life, it is consciously engaging with the energy within you every day and consistently building your circuitry. As you bring in and anchor to high-frequency energy, you dissolve the blockages that hold you back and activate the parts of your body and consciousness that have not yet awakened.

Make the energy codes practices a constant and consistent part of your everyday life so that your mind's default mode is to follow your energy rather than defend the stories from your ego. Integrating your Protective Personality into your Soulful Self won't happen instantly, but practicing regularly will develop the momentum that will take you to your goal.

Key Takeaway: Make the Energy Code practices part of your daily schedule to live your best life.

Use your work breaks to do a few mindful yoga poses. If your work entails sitting for long periods, yoga can awaken your body and allow high-frequency energies to flow through it. Start by practicing one pose for one chakra each day of the week. You can also scan your body while you are on your break to see which chakra you need to focus on, then do the yoga pose for it.

Alternatively, you can do the Morter March or any of the breathwork practices described in the energy codes while you are on a break. If you have thirty minutes to spare, you can do the breathwork exercises for the first ten minutes to get your energy flowing then sit in silent meditation for the remainder of the time. Each of these practices brings more life into your core and unifies your energies.

Most importantly, keep monitoring the flow of your energy throughout the day. Sensations that run through your body are signals from your Soulful Self telling you where you need to bring your focus. When someone charges your emotions, commit to resolve the friction through your energy field rather than your mind. Squeeze the area where you feel the sensation and breathe through it. Remember that this is the fastest and easiest way to expand your consciousness.

CHAPTER 12: LIFE ON THE FRONT SIDE: LIVING AS THE SOULFUL SELF

Your Soulful Self has access to more knowledge than your intellect can put together. When you build your circuitry and enhance your flow of energy, you make it easy for your intuitive mind to lead. And when you are living from your Soulful Self, your pure essence flows through and out of you to transform your life and the lives of others.

Key Takeaway: When you are living as your Soulful Self, you are living in awareness of your wholeness and perfection.

When you are living as the Soulful Self, your mind takes the role of observer and facilitator. It stops overthinking and, rather than compete with you, serves you in your journey as it unfolds.

When you are living as the Soulful Self, you are living from a place of total acceptance. You accept that the inner world is the real world, and the outer world is just a projection of this real world. You also accept that everything that happens is for the expansion of your consciousness. You detach yourself from ideas of how things ought to be and come to appreciate that life provides you with exactly what you need to evolve.

You come to trust in your truth, visions, and desire because you know that everything that comes through you is from the soul of the universe. These desires and visions begin to come true as you own them. You draw people in with your presence, and inspirations and resources come with ease because the place you are operating from is uninhibited by space, time, or physicality.

You begin to see love, peace, joy, abundance, and perfect harmony all around you, because your reality is a reflection of your inner world.

EDITORIAL REVIEW

In her new book, *The Energy Codes*, self-styled bio-energetic medicine and quantum field visionary Dr. Sue Morter describes the combination of breathwork, muscle-squeezing techniques, yoga asanas, and diet that people can use to magnify the vital energy within them and become healthier, happier, and more successful.

Writing casually and simply for a lay audience, the founder of the Morter Institute for Bioenergetics makes the case that health and wellbeing depend less on the circumstances of your life and more on the flow of energy in your body. When you clear the energy blockages that hold you back, Morter contends, you can experience healing and transformation faster than you could with medicine and therapy. The first part of the book, which makes up about 30 percent of the book, may sound like a lengthy build-up to the energy codes, but the philosophies that underpin the codes turn out to be as important as the codes themselves.

Readers who are familiar with energy medicine, manifestation, or the chakras and other esoteric traditions of Hinduism will find the practices Morter recommends both practical and useful. Each chapter in the second part of the book has easy, step-by-step guidelines to increase energy flow around each of the seven chakras and create possibilities for healing and living a fuller life. Morter anticipates that some of the practices she recommends may be difficult to follow. She refers readers to her website, drsuemorter.com, which has video tutorials that demonstrate the breathwork, muscle squeezes, and yoga postures described in her book.

Skeptics and the uninitiated, however, may struggle with the veracity of the testimonials she offers as proof of the healing power of energy medicine. Morter reports, for example, that one of her patients' severed fingers regenerated—naturally, without surgery—through the use of a technique that increases energy flow through the body and hands. Morter herself claims to have corrected the painful scoliosis she had since birth through a consistent application of the energy codes.

These reports sound dubious, and it does not help that her claims, as with most of other claims made by alternative medicine practitioners, are anecdotal and not based on repeatable empirical evidence. The few scientific studies Morter mentions merely support the theories that underpin energy medicine. The dots are there—and no one is questioning the dots—but there are no clinical trials to connect them.

Moreover, the occasional attempts to discredit modern medicine and surgery make *The Energy Codes* a contradiction of sorts, because Morter comes out as someone who takes great pride in being a prominent science personality. To the skeptic, Morter's work is a long-shot attempt at merging science with spirituality; a wild gamble at backing two horses in the same race and expecting both to win. Of course, fans and followers of Morter's won't be put off by the lack of scientific backing for her program as many have experienced the benefits of energy healing for themselves firsthand.

Lastly, what *The Energy Codes* lacks in scientific rigor, it makes up for in gritty humanness. Morter, who opens up about the pain of being sexually abused as a child, losing her mother, going through an unpleasant breakup, and being cut out of her father's will, inspires trust with her vulnerability and warmth. Even if you are skeptical as to the efficacy of her program, she speaks to anyone who feels there has to be a better way to be and live.

BACKGROUND ON AUTHOR

Sue Morter is an American author, international speaker, and president and CEO of Morter Institute and Health Center. She has a doctor of chiropractic degree from the Logan College of Chiropractic, which she attended from 1983 to 1986. Her father, Dr. Milton Theodore Morter Jr., was a prominent chiropractic physician and one of the pioneers of energy medicine. Sue Morter helped her father with his work on energy research until his death in 2013.

Since founding the Morter Institute in 1987, Morter has been teaching self-healing techniques, consciousness elevation, and life mastery. The institute serves about 10,000 patients annually. In addition to her practice, Morter takes individuals on yoga and meditation retreats in Indonesia, Peru, Mexico, and across the US.

Morter is also the founder of Soulful Science Productions, a company that produces guided meditation and affirmations for autistic and differently-abled children. She serves on several professional licensing and human service boards globally.

Morter has won several awards for her work in Transformation Leadership. She has also appeared in several documentary films, including *Discover the Gift*, *The Cure is*, and *The Opus*. She is currently based in the city of Carmel in Indiana, USA.

END OF BOOK SUMMARY

*If you enjoyed this **ZIP Reads** publication, we encourage you to purchase a copy of <u>the original book.</u>*

We'd also love an honest review on Amazon.com!

Want **FREE** book summaries delivered weekly? Sign up for our email list and get notified of all our new releases, free promos, and $0.99 deals!

No spam, just books.

Sign up at <u>www.zipreads.co</u>

Made in the USA
Las Vegas, NV
18 June 2022